Imagination is more important than knowledge.
For knowledge is limited, whereas imagination
embraces the entire world.

—Albert Einstein

This journal belongs to

....

THE MINDFULNESS CREATIVITY JOURNAL

THE

MINDFULNESS CREATIVITY

Journal

Artistic Prompts to Relax, Release, and Explore the Wisdom of *You*

Worthy Stokes

Illustrations by Jenny Bowers

ROCKRIDGE PRESS

For the ones who imagine beautiful things.

Interior and Cover Designer: Michael Patti
Art Producer: Samantha Ulban
Editors: Erin Nelson and John Makowski

Illustrations © 2020-21 Jenny Bowers. Author Photo Courtesy of David Genik Photography.

ISBN: Print 978-1-64739-928-3
R0

Beginnings

As a child, I was taught to believe imagination is the most essential life skill and art is a way of being. Raised by an artist who could see energy (my mother) and a PhD wilderness management professional who loved nature (my father), spheres of creativity, interdependent systems, and spiritual inspiration were fastened together at home, wholly interconnected. I grew up with a formative, wide-angle view: Consciousness is art in motion, and sculpting our physical world with attentive presence is deeply meaningful work.

Long before I began to teach meditation, I had been trained to notice my surroundings, appreciate beauty, dream bigger, listen deeper, and learn from all the colors of the world. My father would say everyone needs to explore. My mother would say everyone is an artist. Nowadays, I say the very same things to my clients: "Explore. You are a cosmic artist. Your soul is a sculptor, and this life is your work of art. Find yourself in the eye of your mind. Don't be afraid to color outside of the lines. You matter."

In college, I studied journalism, darkroom printing, and photography (the science of writing with light). In my 20s, I began to focus on meditation. Later, after surviving a brain injury, complicated sensory loss, and a lucid near-death experience in my early 30s, I applied a blend of neuroscience, creativity, and mindfulness to my recovery. In my quest to heal, I became a mystical explorer of inner space. In doing so, I resurrected myself from suicidal ideation, mind-altering grief, and numbing, emotional pain; I traveled through my neurochemistry with an ecstatic, newfound appreciation for vast, neural networks that bind the soma to the soul. My experience with brain trauma transformed my meditation practice—and my teaching style—forever.

I now believe that meditation is a marvelous, creative path—we are alchemists with infinite potential. To pay attention to this human experience and consciously shape it with the power of a creative vision, in a way that is deeply mindful, is a radical experiment. Our inner genius is meant to be known and shared with others. We are born with this knowledge intact, yet, over time, we forget. As we grow older, we face tragedy. Some of us become accustomed to thinking that creativity is only for children, or we grow rigid with disappointment and give up. Years pass before we look around and notice we have been sleepwalking.

IT IS TIME TO WAKE UP

Reclaim your sacred right to harness creativity for the sake of mindful participation in this life. The decision to evolve your true nature is both an act of great self-love and a warmhearted symbol of devotion to our shared experience of interconnectedness; collective transformation is most readily achieved when we, as individuals, choose to consciously evolve. As often as possible, let the art of who you are unbreak your heart. We were made for this work.

—*Worthy Stokes*

How to Use This Journal

Welcome to a journal of awakening. The pages here aim to nourish your inner landscape with spontaneity, joy, and contemplative wellness. The gentle arc of exploration is designed to bring you back to the present moment, again and again.

As you follow these pages in sequential order, or intuitively as inspired, you will learn to practice the art of turning toward the instinct of creativity. You will find a range of offerings here to support your new journey into mindfulness. Pay attention to what inspires you as you explore your deepest self with writing prompts, meditation practices, inspirational quotes, and activities. Open to a warmhearted curiosity as you begin to notice more of your world, practice artistic expression, and attune to your natural awareness; an embodied experience awaits. This is a series of gentle prescriptions for the soul, ones that weave your presence with your potential, fasten your thoughts to the infinite, boundless principles of imagination, and nourish self-expression with creativity in an expansive journey home to your spiritual essence. *Creativity is what you already are. These are some tools to help you express it.*

Mindfulness and Creativity: An Interwoven Path

The practice of mindfulness is an exercise in consciousness whereby you train yourself to apply the contemplative power of your cognition to the intuitive flow of streaming awareness. Imagine your eye as an aperture of a camera lens that views the world in a fixed manner. Your creative life force energy is what you can harness to shift your perspective from a finite point to an open, spacious view. This wider perspective gives way to joy; all that is required of you is the intention to recognize forgotten parts of your inner landscape—the ones you long to reclaim.

To clarify, it is not necessary to be a professional artist or have a background in meditation to embrace the creative wisdom within. A mindful perspective is available to you right now, and it can be engaged with gracious ease, anytime you wish. Gradually, the soulful impetus to solve problems or think broadly about mundane obstacles will expand.

The artful arc of your attention begins with exploration. Your life is your sacred journey, and the call of awakening is a quest for the soul to embody this tapestry of being. Open yourself to a process of intuitive, alchemical meandering and have faith in the miracle that is you.

FLOW STATE

At the intersection of mindfulness and creativity, there is a particular quality of wakefulness often referred to as *flow state*. Flow state is an integrated, holistic experience of consciousness and fluidity. Activities such as journaling, drawing, and creative projects are doorways to access this life energy source. Whenever you activate a flow state with energized focus, you are following the path to a deeper self.

Mindful journaling is an autotelic experience designed to awaken your inner vision to a sense of beingness. We tend to perform and feel our best when work or play (action) is linked effortlessly to presence (awareness). Research consistently shows that the more creative we are, the easier it is to access flow state, which is why a combination of meditation and artistic exercises can be an effective and fun way to train the brain to function optimally. In turn, as flow state becomes more accessible, we naturally become more creative. This cycle eventually creates sustainable, positive changes in our neurobiology such as improved functionality of memory, cognitive flexibility, spatial attention, and more.

Meditation is often discussed in mainstream media as a technique for stilling your thoughts, slowing down, or quieting the mind. Yet high-performing athletes, entrepreneurs, and leadership experts utilize the practice of mindfulness to do just the opposite: harness raw mental energy to think fast and move well for the sake of creative problem-solving and flow-state success.

The more flow you can sense within, the more flow you experience while moving from one moment to the next. As your conscious attention to your inner landscape and your outer environment begins to evolve, you can start to notice an effortless congruency arise with a deep, abiding ease. The practice of mindful awareness while exploring your creative energy with a contemplative lens will, over time, strengthen your connection with your deepest self: emotional shifts become more manageable, the ability to concentrate gets easier, and the quality of your life naturally improves.

ONE MIND AND OUR DEEPEST SELVES

Physics has shown our bodies are made mostly of empty space, and scientists across disciplines are on a never-ending quest to prove a formula for mapping our divinity. In reality, your deepest self defies translation. The true nature of your consciousness is so exquisite and complex, there is no language for it. There is, however, a way to feel its grand emergence.

While some are troubled by such ambiguity, it's important to point out that the elegance of your soul is your personal mystery to interpret. There is no right or wrong way; there is *your* way. So how do you tap into this inner world, the sacred landscape designed just for you?

If you think of your mind as a flexible, diamond-like structure with multiple facets, imagine each particle of your cognitive awareness reflects your spiritual potential. This is then filtered through the material substance of your corporeal form. By some miracle, your nonphysical soul and your physical body are moving together in a prism of space, time, and breath. At the nexus of countless, seemingly disparate atoms that barely touch each other, there is a through line of life force energy that inexorably links you to the unified field of consciousness, otherwise known as One Mind, or absolute reality. This primordial source of luminous intelligence is always within. And you can train yourself to access it, anytime you wish.

THE ROLE OF MEDITATION

With time and practice, you will find yourself capable of holding a spectacular kind of attention that encompasses both the vastness of the absolute field of One Mind and the mundane, sacred work of getting to your next meeting on schedule. The dance of presence is in the space between what we know to be true and what we can imagine with our thinking, beautiful brain.

Creative exercises, when blended with mindfulness, are opportunities to harness your neurological capacity with directive intent. They are a way to feel into the present moment with a sense of authentic joy. And they are a chance to practice the art of looking forward in time with anticipatory hope.

Spaciousness, Illumination, and Joy

The practice of mindful awareness is both a practical life skill and a mystical doorway; as you discover a new experience of your innermost being, you open yourself to a mind-bending joy that exists alongside (not in place of) the various challenges that arise in your everyday routines. Instead of hoping that meditation will cure you, fix others, or erase obstacles you long to escape, it is useful to recognize that meditation is fundamentally about *the illuminating work of finding more space.* As you build space into your day to breathe, create, and think effectively, a tender intimacy with all that exists is bound to expand. At the heart of this spaciousness there is unfathomable potential—to meet yourself and others with such deep, abiding presence is a gift.

Types of Meditation in This Journal

Depending on your needs, you may wish to experiment with the practices, exercises, and techniques explored here in this journal, which are categorized as focused attention or open awareness.

The practice of **focused attention** is a path of zooming in with repetition. Here, your attention on a mundane task is detailed, specific, and narrow because the goal is to train your mind to strengthen its capacity to focus on one thing at a time. This meditation style is especially useful for anyone who feels easily distracted or struggles to be present. The invitation is to connect with the depth of a single detail and relate intimately with your conceptual, temporal reality.

Examples: detailed writing, listening to a song, tasting a cup of tea, repeating a mantra, gazing for long periods of time at a symbol, reflecting on specific moments, and any exercise designed to engage your cognitive ability to pay especially close attention.

In contrast, the practice of **open awareness** is a path of zooming out with gracious ease. Your gaze softens, your attention widens, and there is a spaciousness that arises in your cognitive experience. The practice is less about linear details and more about tapping into your creative flow. As you connect deeply with your inner vastness, the mind's awareness naturally opens, and your normal thinking patterns begin to stretch.

This meditation style is especially useful for anyone who has a tendency to fixate on details or think with some degree of rigidity. An open awareness practice trains you to take a step back and notice what you normally miss: solutions, concepts, or information you would not otherwise see. The invitation is to relate intimately with absolute reality and the abstract nature of your potential. This is where the nonconceptual mind is able to roam freely and rest. This practice encourages a wide-angle view (or an expansive perspective) and allows for fresh ideas to surface. New awareness can emerge gently.

Examples: intuitive dance, visualization exercises that engage your imagination, coloring, humming without specific words, vocal toning, and any practice designed to engage one's cognitive ability—to hold a perspective that differs from usual thinking patterns.

What to Bring to Your Practice

As you look for a match to your meditation style, there are effectively two critical details you need to understand as you begin a practice or deepen your inner work. First, research shows the intention you bring to your practice is as important as the meditation technique itself. Second, in order to activate flow state, the technique you choose to practice must be challenging, but not so challenging that you feel like giving up. Tune in to the space between the subtle tension of learning a new skill and creative fluidity. Pay attention to your joy.

With time and experience, you may find yourself choosing different practices for different reasons and different times. This is great! On some days, you may need to focus your attention more. On other days, you may need to dive into problem-solving with a decidedly abstract view. Meditation is a practice of evolving a conscious relationship with your inner, spiritual terrain, so you may then channel this presence into your relationships with others.

This journey is an adventure in discernment. As you change, so will your practice, and as your practice changes, you, too, will evolve. The joy of a contemplative path is grounded in your work to bring luminosity to the voyage. To practice presence is to choose to be awake for your life.

Without inner change, there can be no outer change.

—angel Kyodo williams

Imagine a sacred space that helps you feel safe, connected, and soulful. What does it look like and feel like? How can you create more sacred spaces in your life?

A WALKING MEDITATION FOR NOTICING BEAUTY

» Set aside time for a leisurely walk through your neighborhood or a place you like to visit.

» Look for interesting objects in your visual field you may not usually notice. There may be a fountain, or you may see the pillars of a building you walk past. Maybe it is the detail of a home, a mural, or a tree.

» As you bring your full sensory awareness to the objects you notice, what is something new that stands out, something you did not ever see before?

» How are you touched by beauty? Where do you feel it, in your body?

Identify ways that you give to the world. Name (or draw) as many as you can.

WAYS THAT YOU
GIVE TO THE WORLD

Who do you love? Draw a star for each of the people you care about and connect the stars to make your own constellation of love. What shape is it?

CONNECTING WITH YOUR STRENGTH

///

» Turn inward to reflect on physical sensations as you relax into a comfortable position for a mindful body scan.

» Connect first with a part of you that feels strong, and, as you do this, think of a color for the part of you that feels good.

» Inhale and exhale gently as you pay attention to this good sensation and to the color of what feels strong. This is called "mindful resourcing."

» Imagine breathing this beautiful strength from the strong parts of your body into the parts of you that carry physical tension or feel weak.

» For additional support, envision yourself surrounded in this color for the next few hours.

Be willing to not know what to do. Just allow yourself to be intuitively inspired by guidance that shows up in every present moment.

—Maryam Hasnaa

RESTING IN OPEN AWARENESS

» Settle into a comfortable seated position and, with your eyes closed, take five gentle, full breaths.

» Feel the places where your body touches the ground. Notice how the entirety of the physical space that is your body makes contact with other surfaces in perfect balance. Gravity holds you.

» Choose one point of contact, maybe the balls of your feet, and focus your attention on the size of this area.

» Then notice the area around this point of contact. Slowly allow your attention to move outward from this point and recognize the vastness.

» Move on to another point of contact, perhaps the tips of your toes. Feel the points of contact between your toes and the ground beneath them. Focus on the size of this space and its relation to the vastness that surrounds it. Rest in this space.

FEELING
NOURISHED

//

» Practice conscious eating with a simple, mindful breathing practice for appreciation the next time you eat.

. . . .

» First, decrease distractions by putting away your phone, sitting down quietly, and designating plenty of time to nourish yourself.

. . . .

» You might want to listen to gentle music or try this with a friend or loved one at home.

. . . .

» Before you eat, take a moment to look at the colors and shapes of what is on your plate and let your eyes feel the simple beauty of seeing.

. . . .

» Throughout your meal, inhale and exhale with ease, and every time you take a new bite of your food, silently say "thank you" (so that no one can hear).

. . . .

» This helps you to cultivate gratitude for what you have and focus attention on a slower pace.

. . . .

A turtle carries its shell on its back. What makes you feel at home within yourself? What do you always have with you? In the shells below, draw or write what you feel your shell of home and belonging looks like.

Worrying can be a healthy reminder about the things that require your attention. Write a list of worries on your mind right now. Circle the ones you can do something about in this moment. Then draw a line through the ones you cannot do anything about, at least at this present time. Choose your biggest circled worry and write down one action step you can take to address it, to regain a greater sense of balance.

....

....

....

....

....

....

....

....

....

....

....

....

....

....

....

....

As you listen to a favorite song or playlist, practice automatic drawing with a pencil for the duration of the music. Let your subconscious mind roam freely.

The only way to live is by accepting each minute as an unrepeatable miracle.

—Storm Jameson

REALIZING YOUR INFINITE POTENTIAL

» Pick a time to go outside.

» Without looking directly at the sun or damaging your eyes, look upward to rest your gaze on the infinite presence of wide, open space.

» Notice any clouds moving; are they slow or fast?

» Breathing naturally through your nose, connect with the quality of your mind that is like this open sky you can see.

» Think of how open your mind can become, how vast your awareness can be.

» Feel your mind as a sky of possibility, fully capable of holding all you can imagine. This sky is your true nature of infinite potential.

Before you leave this Earth, what is one dream you would like to achieve? Set a timer for 5 minutes and write down a dream you can live out in the next 90 days.

RETREAT FROM TECH

» Choose an entire day (24 hours) and commit to taking a mindful social media break.

» Think of this as your own mini tech retreat and have fun!

» That morning, turn off your smartphone and put it in a safe place.

» Commit to not turning it back on until the next morning at the same exact time.

» Throughout the day, notice how often you reach for your phone and, whenever you do, inhale and exhale gently three times.

» Look around your environment and take time to notice your surroundings.

» What colors are there? Who do you see? What does it feel like to disconnect with technology in order to connect more deeply with your life?

» As you go from one moment to the next, what is different? As you prepare for bed, do you notice a difference?

The gift of your presence is a powerful offering. Think of a time when you have given without asking for anything in return. For example, have you volunteered your time to a friend, organization, or mission? How does the act of giving or sharing your time with others make you feel?

....

....

....

....

....

....

....

....

....

....

....

....

....

....

....

....

....

....

EXPERIENCING
YOUR SOUL

//

» Imagine the inner terrain of your heart.

» There is a symbolic place in a physical locale, in the center of your heart, where you can go anytime to connect with sensations of belonging. Take time to rest in this space.

» Start with a few deep breaths. Count off eight breaths, if you can, with your eyes closed or open with a soft gaze.

» Then count backward: 8 – 7 – 6 – 5 – 4 – 3 – 2 – 1.

» There is a part of you that is infinite. Can you feel that presence? It is your soul.

» This is the place you can return to anytime. Where you always belong.

What is the best compliment anyone has ever given you?
How did you feel after hearing this? How often do you
compliment others?

....

....

....

....

....

....

....

....

....

....

....

....

....

....

....

....

....

....

....

Take a moment to tune in to your breath. If your most wise, inner self could give you a message of inspiration right now, what would it say? Write it in the circle below.

Write a thought on each stone. Just for today, let these thoughts settle, as if they are resting on the bottom of a clear lake.

Change is inevitable, and impermanence rules. Every moment is an opportunity to embrace change with curiosity and joy instead of fear. Write down one fear that you can turn into curiosity. Imagine this fear as an adventure into the unknown. What happens when you use the power of your mind to embrace change?

No matter how long the room has been dark, an hour or a million years, the moment the lamp of awareness is lit the entire room becomes luminous. You are that luminosity. You are the clear light.

—Tenzin Wangyal Rinpoche

Diamonds are made by enduring unimaginable pressure. The diamond of your resilience is the culmination of obstacles you overcome. Color in the diamond as you reflect on your innate luminosity.

With as much detail as possible, envision your most sacred dream, either for yourself or for the world. By writing down your authentic hopes, you are able to move closer to your soul's longing.

....

....

....

....

....

....

....

....

....

....

....

....

....

....

....

....

....

....

Your hindrances are the
Ingredients
In the kitchen of your
Liberation.

—*Dr. Larry Ward, The Lotus Institute*

Gaze softly at the dot for 1 to 2 minutes. As you inhale and exhale gently, imagine the color infusing your breath with healing energy.

Take a moment to close your eyes and, without moving a muscle on your face, try to smile inside. This is known as your inner smile. Jot down a few words to describe the nature of your inner smile. Remember these words throughout the day.

....
....
....
....
....
....
....
....
....
....
....
....
....
....
....
....
....
....
....

TAPPING IN TO JOY

(inspired by Dr. Richard P. Brown, professor of psychiatry at Columbia University)

» You can do this meditation seated or standing, with or without music.

» With your hand gently cupped, begin tapping your chest near your collarbone. Allow your fingertips, the full length of your thumb, and the edges and sides of your palm to make contact with your chest.

» Feel the sensation of your chest cavity, the skin, the muscle.

» While tapping, move your hand to the left or right shoulder. As you move down your arm, the parts of your hand that make contact will vary. Continue until you reach your fingers and then tap the opposite direction, up your arm.

» You may repeat tapping this arm or move across your chest to the other arm.

» With both hands, tap lightly on your chest; move down your diaphragm to your stomach. Tap the sides of your stomach and your lower back.

» Tap the front and back of your legs as well.

» Finish by gently shaking your arms. Let them be weightless.

» Notice how your body responds to this type of touch.

Think of a time in your past when you felt deep, inner confidence. As you color the spiral on this page, imagine that same confidence is swirling all around you. If you experience moments of tension or stress, recall these colors and the support of the confidence swirling in and around you.

Your mind is in every cell of your body.

—Candace Pert, PhD

AWAKENING
TO COURAGE

//

» Seated in a comfortable position by a sunny window or in your
regular meditation space, take a few deep breaths.

» Allow yourself to breathe effortlessly. In your mind, review your
recent past and the challenges, big or small, that you responded
to. Praise yourself and recognize the courage you showed in
these moments.

» This courage is with you all the time. Breathe into this courage
and feel it.

» Where does this courage show up physically in your body?
Notice the location and focus your breath here. Feel the physical
presence of this courage. This courage is within you.

» Invite courage to be present. Invite the numerous places on your
body where you feel this courage to be active at once. Let this
courage be a support, a shield as you encounter daily challenges.

Even though I feel
discouraged about _____, I am
confident in my ability to take action.
I can _____ right now!
I believe in my ability to manifest
positive change in _____ as I heal,
transform, and evolve with time.

EFFORTLESS
AWARENESS

//

» Seated or lying down, with your eyes closed or resting gently,
take a few gentle, deep breaths.

....

» Effortlessly, notice the sounds around you. Allow the sounds to
enter your space. Is there a repetitive pattern to the sounds? Are
some sounds closer to you than others? Spend a minute or two
noticing sounds.

....

» Moving on to scents, what do you notice? Are the scents consis-
tent? Faint? Distinct in origin?

....

» Moving on to touch, start with your body's points of contact with
surfaces. Maybe the pressure of gravity or feeling of moving is
interesting. Perhaps you're attuned to your heartbeat or breath.

....

» Can you be effortlessly aware of multiple senses at once? Find
comfort and relaxation in the effortless awareness of your working senses.

....

Sit outside in nature—or an environment with elements of nature—and tune in to your surroundings. Breathe naturally through your nose with your mouth closed so you can inhale the smells all around you. Take a moment to record what you notice and feel, and what arises during this time. How does exercise affect your mood?

....

....

....

....

....

....

....

....

....

....

....

....

....

....

....

....

....

On one feather, write down what you are grateful for. On the other feather, write down what you hope to have more of in your life. These are your feathers of gratitude and action.

MINDFUL GRIEF

///

At times, the opportunities this life presents to you can become heavy with disappointment and grief. It is possible to be joyful and grateful and present with this grief when you make space for it.

» Start slow and gentle. Set aside 5 or 10 minutes for your grief when you can be uninterrupted and in a safe space.

» If you notice your grief showing up strongly at inopportune moments, tell your grief that you will make time for it later. Pick a time and stick to it.

» Once in that intention time, set a timer for 5 or 10 minutes. In a comfortable position invite your grief to be present for the specified time. Say aloud, "Grief, you are invited to be fully present for [X] minutes."

» Breathe gently and remember that you are safe. The timer will bring you back. Thank yourself for the courage to sit fully present with your grief.

Note: Meditation is often not enough for grief. Let meditation be the sustainer, the support, to find additional specialized resources to help you live with your grief.

How has music or art supported you in difficult times? Is there a specific moment that stands out to you when the arts made a noticeable difference in your mood, behaviors, or overall healing journey? For example, does music help you cope with sadness? Does drawing or painting bring you joy? Describe how the energy of creativity makes you feel.

....

....

....

....

....

....

....

....

....

....

....

....

....

....

....

....

....

....

Do you know what joy feels like inside you? Does it flutter or move in some other way? Is it quiet or loud? Next to the butterflies, sketch an image of the feeling of joy—whatever comes to mind! Color the butterflies. As you draw and color, imagine your feelings of joy expand.

Name one thing in your life that you are having difficulty accepting. Imagine what would happen if you stopped resisting and practiced radical acceptance. What would be different?

....

....

....

....

....

....

....

....

....

....

....

....

....

....

....

....

....

....

....

Optimism is the faith that leads to achievement.
Nothing can be done without hope and confidence.

—Helen Keller

In each floating bubble, write a worry. Imagine your worries floating away, as if these concerns are resting in mind bubbles and moving gently through space.

Love your heart. For this is the prize.

—*Toni Morrison*

 Research shows your heart energy expands outward. Draw your heart energy as if it touches others and radiates into the world.

In the first column, write a list of positive characteristics others have said you have. In the second column, write a list of positive characteristics you believe you have. Do you see any words that overlap? Are you able to celebrate these attributes? Own your positive inner view.

Others Said

I Believe

....

....

....

....

....

....

....

....

....

....

....

....

Make a he(art) collage to represent the feelings of love you hold for someone in your life. Add color or doodles. What does your love look like?

SENDING LOVING-KINDNESS INTO THE WORLD

//

» Gently close your eyes, or leave them open with a soft gaze, and imagine floating in space.

» Direct your attention to the entire planet, as if you are seeing the Earth as a blue dot when observed from very far away in outer space.

» Start by sending yourself a giant hug while floating outside gravity. You may wrap your arms around yourself, resting your hands on your shoulders or your sides.

» Allow all of the love and goodwill you have to flow from your arms and hold you. Take three or four breaths here.

» Now move this energy of loving-kindness into other people, like the residents and neighbors in your community with whom you wish to share this embrace.

» Now, imagine your entire city enveloped in the space of gentle loving-kindness. Then your state, your country, and finally the entire planet is held in your embrace as you share love.

Bring an energy of alertness and aliveness to your day by turning your attention to your breath. Anytime you feel overwhelmed by your emotions or thoughts, you can change your breathing pattern and use your breath as a support to bring a state change to your neurobiology. Set a timer for 2 minutes. Without exerting effort, close your mouth and breathe naturally through your nose. What is different about your thoughts? How do you feel? Jot down some notes or a key phrase to help remind you to breathe whenever you experience anxiety or stress.

....

....

....

....

....

....

....

....

....

....

....

....

....

....

....

....

You and I are the force for transformation in the world. We are the consciousness that will define the nature of the reality we are moving into.

—Ram Dass

Make your own color wheel by choosing a color and matching it with a feeling. Then, color in the wheel.

FEELING   COLOR

_____ _____

_____ _____

_____ _____

_____ _____

_____ _____

_____ _____

There are multiple ways to integrate practicing gratitude in your everyday life. How do you practice gratitude? What ways could you add to this practice?

INTEGRATING GRATITUDE

//

» Reflect on the day ahead of you, or if you are practicing at the
end of the day, the day behind you.

....

» Make a list of key moments in your day. Pick a moment from
your list and recall what preceded that moment. It may help to
close your eyes when doing this.

....

» What are you remembering? Who are you remembering?

....

» Take time to express gratitude for this moment and the people or
objects involved.

....

Write a sacred prayer for inner prosperity and outer wellness.

....

....

....

....

....

....

....

....

....

Write a haiku to describe your closest friend or someone special to you. Here are the rules for writing a haiku: The entire poem consists of just three lines, with 17 syllables in total. The first line is five syllables. The second line is seven syllables. The third line is five syllables.

Five syllables

Seven syllables

Five syllables

Reflect on people in your life who help you feel safe, cherished, and seen. What characteristics do you see in them? Which of these qualities can you choose to embody right now? Take a few moments to write two to three ways you are able to adopt the characteristics you admire so much and write an intention to carry this love forward.

Next to each bird, write a message of peace and imagine the messages being carried into the world.

Do ordinary things with extraordinary love.

—Mother Teresa

Make a list of places that feel sacred to you. Travel through space and time to draw your spiritual pilgrimage.

BECOMING
THE WITNESS

» Find a safe, comfortable space where you can sit or stand for a few minutes or more.

» Allow your focus to be expansive and gentle, acknowledging your periphery, what is right in front of you, and the space around you.

» When your gaze settles naturally on a spot, soften your breath— breathe effortlessly. Imagine, this time, that your eyes are breathing.

» View all that is in front of you without shifting your gaze. Be gentle. Allow your visual surroundings to simply be, as you practice seeing from your mind's eye.

» Be still and aware of what is there.

» The point is to feel your surroundings for a time without effort, without judgment.

In order to be ▓▓▓▓▓▓▓ or ▓▓▓▓▓▓▓▓

I will need to: ▓▓▓▓▓▓▓▓▓▓

MOVIE DIRECTOR

Write or draw something important to the "movie" of your life. If you are the director of your spiritual journey, what is essential to your story?

Write a letter to yourself at age 16. What advice would you give your 16-year-old self to help them follow a dream?

COMING HOME
TO YOURSELF

//

» With your eyes softly closed, direct your attention to the space around your body.

» In your mind's eye, envision a shape; notice the first image that appears.

» Notice if the shape has a color, or choose a color that soothes you.

» Imagine yourself stepping into that shape and sealing it so nothing can get in. This is your inner space.

» Rest inside this shape, where you are surrounded by space, and breathe without effort. With every breath you might connect more deeply with this inner terrain, where you always belong to yourself.

» When you complete this meditation journey, give yourself a hug. Hold yourself for a few moments. Notice what it feels like to realize that you are able to go within, to rest in a place that only you can reach, anytime you wish.

Draw colors and shapes to express how you feel after meditating.

HOW MEDITATION FEELS

The path of loving-kindness is a spiritual journey that encompasses a deep regard for all sentient beings. How do you define loving-kindness? Write a list of simple, nonverbal ways or specific actions you can take to show loving-kindness toward others—and yourself—in small moments. Practice this throughout the day and, before you go to sleep, reflect on how it made you feel.

....

....

....

....

....

....

....

....

....

....

....

....

....

....

....

....

....

Put your phone in a place where you cannot see it. Prepare for sleep or deep relaxation by coloring the mandala. As you gently move through the motions, feel yourself getting lighter and lighter.

An awake heart is like a sky that pours light.

—Hafiz

Draw a picture of your soul, or your spiritual essence, inside the circle of light. What does the nonphysical part of you look like?

PULSE OF GENTLE PRESENCE

» Pick a song that is slow-paced and comforting, gentle.

» Choose to practice this seated, lying down, or standing up.

» As you tune in to the music, move small parts of your body gently, in synchronicity with the beat and pulse of the sounds you hear. Let your auditory awareness guide you.

» Begin with moving your fingers up and down or make shapes with your hands. Be intuitive.

» Practice gentle movements like flexing your toes and relaxing your jaw.

» Stretch or dance very slowly.

» The objective is to let your thoughts fall away and feel into self-guided movement.

The path of generosity and minimalism involves letting go. Make a list of things you are ready to give away.

....

....

....

....

....

....

....

....

....

....

....

....

....

....

....

....

....

....

....

....

Compassion is not a virtue—it is a commitment.
It's not something we have or don't have—it's
something we choose to practice.

—Brené Brown

How do you show people you care about that you're truly listening while they're talking? Write about what your body language looks like when you are truly present, how another person's voice sounds, whether your breath is fast or slow. Are you able to practice mindful listening more often? Write a mindful commitment reminding yourself to slow down to hear what someone is trying to tell you.

Choose a photograph you took recently. Turn the picture upside down. Draw the shapes and lines you see while letting your mind wander.

Feeling inspired by others is an important part of aligning your mind with hope, creativity, and intention. Name a painter, writer, dancer, scientist, or artist you admire and wish you could have dinner with. What do you notice about this person that is so inspiring? What does this person inspire *you* to do that maybe you're afraid to try?

....

....

....

....

....

....

....

....

....

....

....

....

....

....

....

....

....

....

ACTIVATING YOUR INNER STRENGTH

//

» Seated upright, or lying down, close your eyes and imagine a ray of light entering through the top of your head, traveling to the soles of your feet.

» As this light travels through your body, an impenetrable protective sphere grows from within you and encloses you in absolute safety.

» This sphere is your inner strength. It manifests itself to remind you that if you pause, for just a moment, and take a few breaths, strength will emerge.

Write or draw three things you have accomplished in the circles. Consider this the art of saying "yes!"

DANCING WITH GRIEF

» Where do you feel grief in your body? If you could match this grief with a song, what would that song be?

» Tune in to sensations of grief as you listen to music that reflects your innermost feelings. Dance your way through the pain.

» Don't try to release grief or banish it from your field of awareness. Feel the way it becomes a part of who you are, how it inspires you, and tune in to the way it moves.

Take a moment to travel into the labyrinth of your mind, perhaps while listening to gentle music. With a pencil, draw a line into the labyrinth and don't let your pencil leave the paper. Gently, with intention and ease, draw your way through the puzzle.

ENTERING YOUR SECRET GARDEN OF KNOWING

» Gently soften your gaze or close your eyes for this simple visualization that enhances creativity and inspires inner awareness. Imagine yourself in a secret garden that only you have access to.

» In the center, imagine there is a mystical tree with deep, strong roots and a tall, expansive canopy that stretches into the sky of your mind.

» As you connect with the easy, natural space all around you, what do you see? Imagine this secret garden holds all of your wisdom from all of your lived experiences, and you can access this wise part of you anytime you wish.

» As you go about your day, return to this image whenever you wish to remind yourself of your inner knowing.

Imagine who you will be one year from now. Take a moment to close your eyes and envision your most heartfelt wish for your future self. Draw or write what you see.

DISSOLVING TENSION
WITH YOUR BREATH

//

» Lying on your back with your legs bent at the knees, rest your
legs at a right angle over a chair or sofa, or in another comfortable lying or seated position, exhale fully, and on the inhale say,
"Inhale, two, three, four, five, six," and then "Exhale, two, three,
four, five, six."

» Repeat this for 5 minutes.

» If your attention drifts, you can direct your breath to different
parts of your body. Maybe there is discomfort in your lower back.
Use your inhale and exhale to brush over and through your mus-
cles, washing away tension, releasing discomfort.

» Do this practice once every day. If you are able to do this multiple times per day, you will bring enormous relief to your
nervous system.

» If 6-second breaths are uncomfortable, count to 5, starting with
breaths that are manageable.

What makes up your inner world? Draw or color your inner landscape, the place within where you can rest when the outer world feels overwhelming.

FEELING THE MEDICINE OF JOY

//

» Think of a time when a smile covered you, when laughter
erupted from inside you or a happy dance was called for.
When that feeling of joy was so strong that your body reflexively
responded.

» Bring this moment into focus. Breathe in this moment with your
full sensory awareness.

» Feel your joy.

My daily self-care plan includes:

1 ___

2 ___

3 ___

Wholeness is what we naturally desire. What do you need to feel whole? Draw or write your answer in the center of the circle, connecting the broken lines as you imagine your wholeness emerging from within.

Often when we practice acceptance, we focus on accepting a painful moment or circumstance. But did you know that radical acceptance can be applied to joy, too? Take a moment to reflect on how much space you create in your life for feelings of joy. What brought you joy today?

TAKING UP SPACE

» You are a unique, special, and integral gift to the amazing experience of humanity. Right now. And in every moment.

» You deserve to be as big as possible with your dreams, your insights, and your perspective.

» Choose a space that you would like to bring more of yourself to. Maybe it is a social group, your team meetings at work, or your family.

» Visualize yourself in one of these spaces. You are fully present and confident. You are showing up big, not small. You radiate with all that is special about you.

» How do you feel, now, in this space? Locate this feeling. Remember this feeling.

» Spend 5 to 10 minutes with this feeling in the different spaces that you want to show up bigger in. Remembering the feeling will help you take up the space you deserve.

Imagine you have an inner superhero. If your inner superhero had a special shield for protection, what would it look like?

Neuroscientists have discovered that when you ask the brain to meditate, it gets better not just at meditating, but at a wide range of self-control skills, including attention, focus, stress management, impulse control, and self-awareness.

—Kelly McGonigal, PhD

As you color the mandala, breathe mindfully and visualize your creative energy as a mandala of infinite possibility. Take a moment to recognize the simplicity of this meditative experience.

6-COUNT BREATHING
FOR ANXIETY

//

» Resting comfortably in a seated position or lying down, bring
  awareness to your breath.

....

» Gently relax your jaw and rest your eyes softly on a focus
  point nearby.

....

» Inhale with your mouth, and exhale through your nose.

....

» As you inhale, count to 6. Then begin to exhale.

....

» As you exhale, count to 6. Then begin to inhale.

....

» Repeat this for as long as you feel comfortable or for a minimum
  of 5 minutes.

....

In the first sky box, draw what the weather looks like in your mind right now. In the second space, draw what you would like the weather to look like in your mind.

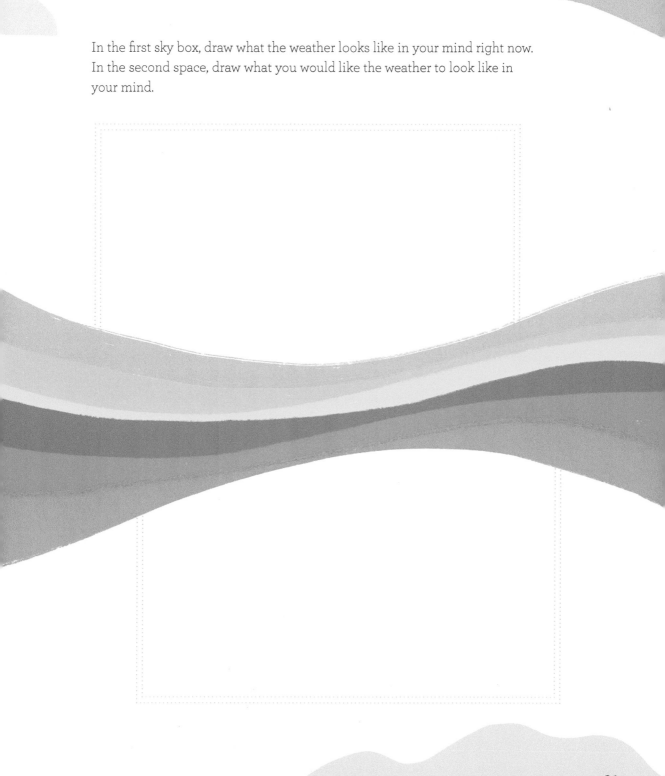

The miracle is not to walk on water. The miracle is to walk on the green earth, dwelling deeply in the present moment and feeling truly alive.

—Thich Nhat Hanh

LEAVING BEHIND

What patterns do you need to leave behind to become more mindful in your relationships?

....

....

....

....

....

....

....

....

....

....

....

WALKING TOWARD

What patterns do you need to learn to become more mindful?

....

....

....

....

....

....

....

....

....

....

....

Write a love letter to your soul. What does
it need to hear? If nothing comes to mind, try
writing a loving letter to your 5-year-old self
and celebrate your inner child.

Some cultures use beads to count prayers, or jewelry to symbolize faith. Write a prayer for each of the beads below.

Name three people who have touched your life with their kindness, generosity, or love. Write them each a short note of appreciation. If you feel compelled, send the note to each person.

According to author Gary Chapman, the five love languages are: words of affirmation, quality time, acts of service, physical touch, and receiving gifts. Each one is a way of expressing love. See if you can describe your love language in your own words. When do you feel loved? How do you show your love?

....

....

....

....

....

....

....

....

....

....

....

....

....

....

....

....

....

....

Describe three to five character traits you liked about yourself as a child. Do you still embody those traits? Why or why not?

....

....

....

....

....

....

....

....

....

....

....

....

....

....

....

....

....

....

Think of a lighthouse and how it shines for boats in a storm, how it supports navigation in difficult seas. Draw or sketch a lighthouse and boat as you reflect on the following:

Are you a boat?   *Are you a lighthouse?*   *Perhaps you are both.*

When you surrender to the natural process of grieving, you can find deep meaning in broken places. What is breaking your heart? Sit with that for a moment. Write a poem in honor of your grief. Hold this message with real tenderness. Befriend your sadness as often as you can.

I contain multitudes.

—Walt Whitman

Kind self-talk is important to your well-being. Write down three positive affirmations or encouraging statements you tell yourself.

Imagine you are a famous speaker or a renowned author about to give a speech about an amazing, life-changing moment in your life. The emcee introducing you is reading your bio to a crowd of 1,000 people. Write the bio the emcee would read to the crowd. How does it feel to witness yourself as someone else? In what way do you inspire others?

....

....

....

....

....

....

....

....

....

....

....

....

....

....

....

....

....

....

How do you nourish your mind, body, and soul? Draw, doodle, or use words to fill in each category. Do you see any overlap?

MIND

SOUL

BODY

What creative expression inspires you most and why? Can you find a way to leave space and time in your schedule for this creative expression in your life?

....
....
....
....
....
....
....
....
....
....
....
....
....
....
....
....
....
....
....

Are you in the right garden, metaphorically speaking, to grow? Where do you shine, evolve, and bloom?

....

....

....

....

....

....

....

....

....

....

....

....

....

....

....

....

....

....

....

On each petal, write in the names of people or ideas that are important to you.

EXPANDING YOUR HEART WISDOM

//

» Rest in a seated position or lying down.

» With your mouth closed, inhale and exhale naturally, without effort.

» Place both hands on your heart so they are resting comfortably.

» With your eyes open or closed, focus your attention on the breath.

» As you inhale, feel the wisdom within your heart expand inward.

» As you exhale, feel the wisdom within your heart expand outward.

» As you continue this practice, notice the wave of heart-centered wisdom touching both your inner landscape and your outer reality.

Write down a positive character trait other people see in you. Celebrate this.

I am ....

GETTING GROUNDED
WITH EASE

//

» You might be surprised how grounding it can feel to be seated on the floor inside your home or sitting outside on the grassy earth in beautiful weather.

....

» Prepare a cup of tea and sit comfortably on the floor or ground, where babies and small children spend so much of their time.

....

» As you sip your tea, notice how your breath naturally settles and whether this physical contact with your body closer to the floor or ground makes a noticeable difference.

....

» Sometimes feeling more grounded is as simple as being on the ground!

....

You are a tree grounded with strong roots. What do your branches and leaves look like? Feel free to unleash your creativity! There are no rules here.

Draw or describe in a poem what you can see with your mind as you gaze at your surroundings and rest in a gentle, visual awareness of what is in your field of vision. Instead of jumping to a judgment about what you see, simply notice what you see. Record it. See if you can experience the neutral feeling of equanimity as you witness your environment from a position of calm, abiding presence.

In each heart below, write a word and add a color to express the way you share your love with others. How do you share your heartfelt nature?

Are you able to recall a time you felt truly courageous? Close your eyes and inhale courage. Can you notice a difference in how you feel when you mindfully breathe in a quality to expand its presence? Write a description of the way courage feels inside you. Tune in to this breath of courage and this feeling whenever you feel depleted.

Draw an image of your inner courage.

CENTERING
IN SAFETY

- » With your eyes open or closed, repeat four times: I am safe. I am safe. I am safe. I am safe.

- » What is your anxiety calling to your attention? See if you can identify its source. Is there a challenge you are in the process of responding to? Is there something you are avoiding? Are you feeling generalized anxiety that has a large, strong, or unclear presence?

- » Thank your nervous system for working tirelessly to keep you safe, for bringing this issue to your attention.

- » Tell your nervous system that you are going to reflect on this for a few moments with no goal or pressure to solve this issue.

- » Above all, remember: Right now, you are safe.

Write a list of things you can do to construct a more mindful space somewhere in your life, so you can enhance inner peace and enjoy the present moment more easily.

When you feel overwhelmed, who shines for you? Sketch that person.
What makes them stand out?

Look around the room and name one thing you can see, hear, smell, touch, and taste. Describe what you notice when you practice five-sense awareness. If you feel inspired, write a brief poem using what you recorded.

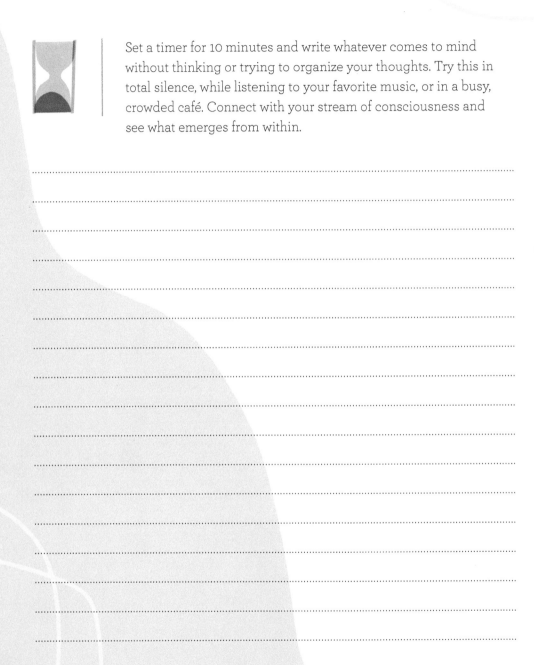

Set a timer for 10 minutes and write whatever comes to mind without thinking or trying to organize your thoughts. Try this in total silence, while listening to your favorite music, or in a busy, crowded café. Connect with your stream of consciousness and see what emerges from within.

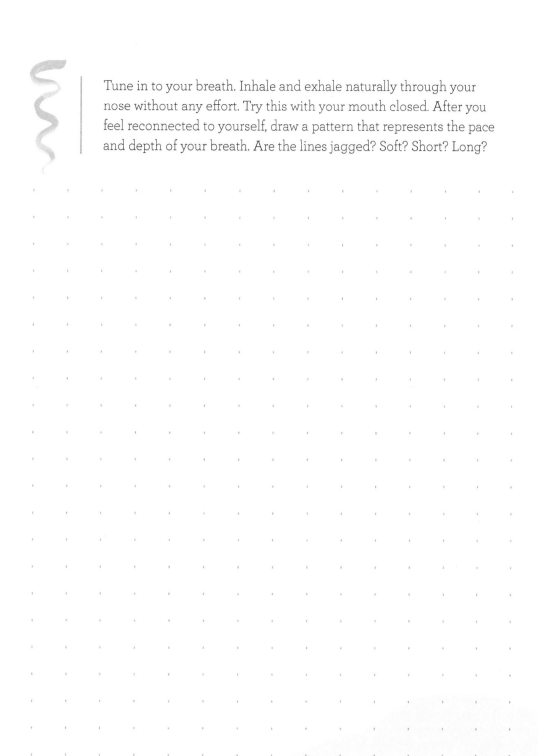

Tune in to your breath. Inhale and exhale naturally through your nose without any effort. Try this with your mouth closed. After you feel reconnected to yourself, draw a pattern that represents the pace and depth of your breath. Are the lines jagged? Soft? Short? Long?

I intend to
leave behind . . .

I intend to
become . . .

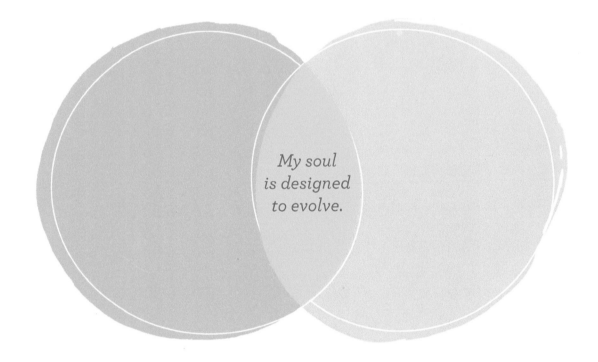

*My soul
is designed
to evolve.*

As adults, we often lose our playful attention. Think of your younger self or your favorite way to play as a child. Spurts of joyful play can be a powerful mindfulness practice! What activity brought you joy? Regardless of how silly it might seem, schedule a time to play and do what you remember loving so much.

....

....

....

....

....

....

....

....

....

....

....

....

....

....

....

....

....

....

VOCAL TONING

//

» In a comfortable, seated position, take three gentle breaths. On the third breath, exhale into a soft hum so that you experience vibration.

» With each exhale, experiment with creating vibrations of various tones. Stay with the tone that feels nourishing.

» Deepen your inhale and extend the sound of your voice, effortlessly.

» Be gentle and loving with yourself.

» How does this feel? Notice the vibrations the tones create.

» Focus the vibration on different parts of your body that need it most, that feel good when filled with the sound and vibration you are creating.

» Different tones may feel better on certain parts of the body.

» You can move in a smooth flow—from the forehead, to the back of the head, to the neck, and then to the shoulders.

In some traditions there are prayer flags or ways to record your prayers in a visual display. What would your prayer flag look like? Draw symbols that are meaningful to you at this phase in your life. As you color in your flags, imagine your prayer going out into the world.

On each flower, write a word for the wisdom you have gained from your lived experiences. Then, choose a color for each wisdom gift. This bouquet represents your inner wisdom in bloom.

Imagine yourself as an older person and tune in to a gentle, radical acceptance of the brevity of this life. Take a moment to acknowledge that one day you will pass. If you put yourself there, what might your future self tell you about the present moment? Write down the advice that comes to mind. Reflect on this wisdom as often as you can.

....

....

....

....

....

....

....

....

....

....

....

....

....

....

....

....

....

Draw or sketch a self-portrait. What do you love about yourself? Practice gratitude for each of your features.

Meditation supports your effort to tap into the power of your dreams and future potential. Write three ways you can use mindfulness, or the creative process, to help you cultivate trust for your inner journey as you continue on your lifelong exploration of the self and the world around you.

Adaptation Guide for Differences in Mobility and Sensory Awareness

This journal is meant to be an inclusive, warmhearted invitation to practice creative, mindful presence with sincere attention to what is comfortable, where you feel strong, and how you need to move with the physical and sensory abilities to which you have direct access. This is a strength-based journal. In other words, the invitation is to resource from within, as often as necessary. Rather than fixating on what your body cannot physically manage, orient your conscious attention to what is possible.

Your brain is responsive to direction, and by acknowledging your natural abilities (while also choosing to celebrate or actively engage them), you are better able to *harness the sensory capacity and physical mobility you already have*, and flow state becomes more readily available. For those of us who practice meditation while surrounded by ableism in areas of language, posture, instruction, and technique, it is essential to feel confident in one's effort to adapt. Remember, you are the expert on what your body needs.

Every meditation practice in this journal can be adapted to your unique abilities, which may vary. These adaptations are general in nature; feel free to create your own. Here is a list of five potential changes you might wish to experiment with or make as you dive into meditation:

1. **Replace One Sense with Another Sense**

   ◆ **Example:** If the practice asks you to use a sense you are missing, try to adapt the practice so it can be done with the sense(s) you do have.

2. **Change Your Position Whenever Necessary**

   ◆ **Example:** If the practice asks you to sit, stand, or walk, and you have difficulty with one or more of these mobility options, adapt the practice so it can be done with the mobility you do have.

3. **Use Your Own Language and Trust Yourself**

   ◆ **Example:** If a word, sentence, feeling, or metaphor does not resonate with you, cross it out and use language that does. Your language of healing matters.

4. **Tune in to Your Breath with Gentle Kindness**

   ◆ **Example:** If breathing is laborious or challenging, tune in to the breathing capacity to which you have access. Sips of air can be gentle, effective, and deeply nourishing.

5. **Practice Compassion with Chronic Illness**

   ◆ **Example:** If you are physically weak, experience chronic or sporadic neurofatigue, or struggle with unpredictable symptoms, practice metta meditation and focus inward. Self-love heals.

About the Author

 **Worthy Stokes** is a HeartMind® Meditation teacher and author. Her warm, personable teaching style reflects an embodied spiritual perspective that is grounded in years of advanced contemplative practice. Her guided meditations have touched thousands across the world. Learn more about her at www.WorthyStokes.com.